GEO-GAMI
PAPER PACK

BASIC FOLD INSTRUCTIONS PLUS 900 PAGES OF ORIGAMI PAPER

STERLING INNOVATION
New York

STERLING INNOVATION
New York

An Imprint of Sterling Publishing
387 Park Avenue South
New York, NY 10016

Cover design: Gavin Motnyk

Geometric patterns: Dover publications, Inc.
Second, third and fourth patterns courtesy of
Keith Hagan Design. Used with permission.

ISBN 978-1-4351-5079-9

Distributed in Canada by Sterling Publishing
c/o Canadian Manda Group, 165 Dufferin Street
Toronto, Ontario, Canada M6K 3H6
Distributed in the United Kingdom by GMC Distribution Services
Castle Place, 166 High Street, Lewes, East Sussex, England BN7 1XU
Distributed in Australia by Capricorn Link (Australia) Pty. Ltd.
P.O. Box 704, Windsor, NSW 2756, Australia

For information about custom editions, special sales, and premium and corporate purchases,
please contact Sterling Special Sales at 800-805-5489 or specialsales@sterlingpublishing.com.

Manufactured in China

2 4 6 8 10 9 7 5 3 1

www.sterlingpublishing.com

CONTENTS

Origami Symbols

VALLEY FOLD:
Fold paper forward

When you open paper that has been valley-folded, you will see a concave crease that bends inward like a groove, or valley. This is called a valley crease.

MOUNTAIN FOLD:
Fold paper backward

When you open paper that has been mountain-folded, you will see a convex crease that bends outward—it has a little peak you can pinch. This is called a mountain crease.

Fold toward you (valley fold) and in direction of arrow.

Fold away from you (mountain fold) and in direction of arrow.

Fold and unfold

Insert

Unfold

Cut along line

Curve paper (soft crease)

X-ray view

	Turn model over from one side to the other		

 Rotate paper one half turn (top of model will rotate to bottom)

 Scale of drawing enlarges

 Rotate paper one quarter turn (top of model will rotate to side)

 Repeat here

 Rotate paper one eighth turn (top of model will rotate to side)

6-8 ↦ Repeat step 6 through 8 here

 Match the dots

90° ▽ Form a right angle

▶ Push here

○ Hold here

Raw Edge

Crease

Folded Edge

Double Raw Edge

Back Layer

Front Layer

5

Basic Folds

BOOK FOLD

Fold one side edge over to lie on opposite side edge.

DIAPER FOLD

Fold one corner to lie over opposite corner.

CUPBOARD FOLD

Fold two opposite parallel sides towards each other to meet at center.

ICE CREAM CONE FOLD

Fold two adjacent sides to meet at center.

HOUSE ROOF FOLD

Fold two adjacent corners to meet at center.

BLINTZ FOLD

Fold all four corners to meet at center.

Note: Although less easily recognizable, the crease pattern for a sideways ice cream cone fold is still called an "ice cream cone fold." The same is true for all the basic folds.

Still an ice cream cone fold.

Still a book fold.

Still a cupboard fold.

Reverse Folds

INSIDE REVERSE FOLD

In order for you to perform a reverse fold, your model or portion of model should have a front layer, a back layer, and a folded edge or spine connecting the two layers. In a reverse fold, an end of this double layer of paper is turned either into itself (inside reverse fold) or around itself (outside reverse fold).

1 You may wish to prepare your paper first by performing a simple valley fold that will serve as a precrease.

2 Check to be sure this is the shape you would like the paper to ultimately take, then unfold.

3 Spread the layers of your paper apart. Apply pressure (push in) at the mountain folded edge (spine) until it changes to a valley fold. At the same time, the precreases you made earlier will both become mountain folded edges.

4 This shows the inside reverse fold in progress. Keep applying pressure to end of paper until model can be flattened.

5 One end of your double layer is now "sandwiched" between the front and back layers.

OUTSIDE REVERSE FOLD

Again, starting with front and back layers connected by a "spine," you can "wrap" one end around both layers, as if turning a hood onto your head.

1 Mark the place where you want the fold to be (precrease). Unfold.

2 Spread the layers apart and wrap end around outside of model.

3 Press flat.

Folding Hints

- It is usually easier to fold paper on a hard surface such as a table.

- Fold as neatly and as accurately as you can.

- If the paper you are using is colored or patterned on one side only: origami directions usually specify which side should be facing up when you begin folding. If this is not indicated, it is usually safe to begin with the white side of the paper facing you.

- It is usually easier to fold paper by bringing an edge from the lower part of the paper up. If you find it easier to fold this way and directions indicate a side-to-side or downward fold, you can always rotate your paper so that the direction of the fold is now upward, and then fold. After folding, reposition your paper so that it looks like the next step in the diagram.

- It is usually easier to make a valley fold in your model than to make a mountain fold. A valley fold becomes a mountain fold when you turn your paper over, so if a diagram indicates to make a mountain fold, you may choose to turn the paper over and make a valley fold. When you turn your paper back to the right side, you will see the desired mountain fold.

- Origami diagrams are usually drawn as if the paper were held loosely rather than pressed flat. This slightly three-dimensional representation is used to give you information about the different layers of paper. If you see a slight gap between edges in a diagram, this would disappear if model were pressed flat.

- In general, your paper should be folded right to an edge or crease, *without* leaving a gap, unless otherwise indicated in the written instructions.

Fold a Masu Box

BOX BOTTOM

1 Begin with the colored side of the square facing up. Book fold and unfold (twice): fold and unfold the square in half in both directions. If you do not want these creases to show on your finished box, crease only near the side edges of the square and leave the middle uncreased. Each long "pinch" should be approximately one-fourth the length of one side.

2 Turn your paper over to the white side. Blintz fold: use the creases from step 1 as a guide to fold all four corners to the center.

3 Cupboard fold and unfold: bring the top and bottom edges inward to meet at the center. Crease sharply and unfold.

4 Cupboard fold and unfold: bringing the right and left sides inward to met at the center. Crease sharply and unfold.

5 Unfold the top and bottom triangular flaps.

6 Refold on the existing creases that connect the far dots. Crease sharply and then partially unfold so that the two flaps stand at a right angle to the rest of the model. They form two sides of your box.

7 For this step you will be folding simultaneously on three existing creases: push inward on the small mountain-fold creases where the color and white meet. At the same time, valley-fold on the crease that connects these two mountain folds.

8 You should now have your box. Grasp the long tab that sticks up and pull it down and inside the box so that it lines the inside of the box.

9 Repeat step 8 on the other open end of your box.

10 Reinforce the creases on the finished box.

BOX LID

11 Use a square the same size as the square you used for the Masu Box. Follow the instructions for the box but replace steps 3 and 4 with the following:

12 Fold the bottom edge up to lie approximately 1/8" below the center. The size of the gap may vary from 1/16" to 3/16", depending on the thickness of the paper you are using. Crease sharply and unfold. Repeat on all four sides on the blintzed square. Continue from step 5 of the box. Fit the finished lid over the box bottom.

OPTIONAL BOX "TRICKS":

• To keep the four flaps that line the inside of your box from "popping" up, lift the flaps up for a moment and place a small piece of tape, sticky side up, in the center of the box. Replace the flaps so that they stick to the tape and also cover it so it is hidden from view.

• For an extra-sturdy box, cut a piece of cardboard to fit in the bottom. Unfold the box back to step 7 and insert the cardboard under the two bottom flaps. Then refold the box and the cardboard will be hidden.